By E-mail with Love

by Jed Mannheimer
illustrated by Mark Elliott

HOUGHTON MIFFLIN BOSTON

September

To: ASmith@worldwork.com

Hi, Dad! How are you? I set up my new computer today. It isn't as good as yours, but it works. Now we can send e-mails to each other. Isn't that great?

Mom is reading right now. She doesn't miss the city. She likes her new job at the library. I don't like anything, but it is pretty here. We live next to a lake!

I miss you and I miss my friends too. Tomorrow is my first day at my new school. I'm worried because I don't know anyone! E-mail me soon.

Love, Melissa

To: Melissa@eduplace.edu

Hi, Sweetie! I loved your e-mail. Don't worry about the new school. It'll be a great experience. You'll make a lot of new friends. Do you like your teacher?

I have a new e-mail address at home. Now it will be easier for us to keep in touch.

Love, Dad

To: Dad123@homeplace.com

My teacher's name is Ms. Lovejoy. I like her but she wants us to read a lot. She wants us to go to the library when we have free time. I wish we had computers in the library.

Hey, you sell computers! Can you talk to the librarian, Mr. Smitz? He is very nice. Maybe the school could buy computers from your company at a discount. Then I would love to go to the library every day!

Love, Melissa

To: Melissa@eduplace.edu

Hi, Sweetie! I would be happy to talk to Mr. Smitz about the computers. But I'm not sure about the discount. Please give him my phone number at work. By the way, Ms. Lovejoy is right. You should go to the library to read. And by the way, you can read at home too!

Love, Dad

To: Dad123@homeplace.com

That was not very funny. But I love you anyway, Melissa

October

To: Dad123@homeplace.com

Here is some news: Mom and I had a lot of fun today. When she came to get me at school, she gave me a new pair of ice skates. She said the lake will freeze soon. Then I can go ice skating. It is already getting cold.

Mom and I went to the lake. We saw a family of ducks. Did I tell you about them? They are so beautiful! The male duck is brown with a green head and red eyes! Mom said they're called wood ducks. I'm going to use my computer to find out more about them. Tomorrow I'll go to the library to look for books about wood ducks. It will give me something to do. I still don't have any friends here.

Love, Melissa

To: Melissa@eduplace.edu

Sweetie, don't worry about the other kids. They are surprised to have a smart, pretty girl like you in their class. When they know you, they will like you. You will have many friends soon. Just wait and see. Believe me, because I am right!

Love, Dad

To: Dad123@homeplace.com

Today was Columbus Day and school was closed. Mom and I went to the skating rink in the afternoon with my new friend Katy and her mom. I put on my new ice skates. We had a lot of fun! When the lake freezes, we will all go ice skating there. The ducks fly south in the winter, so they won't be at the lake. Mom says they will come back in the spring.

Love, Melissa

To: Melissa@eduplace.edu

Sweetie, I can't wait to see you with your new skates! Bring them with you when you visit me. We can go ice skating here in the city.

Mr. Smitz called me today at the office. We talked about computers. He said the school can buy twelve computers for the library. When I drive you home after your visit, I will meet with Mr. Smitz, the principal, and some teachers. Does that make you happy?

Love, Dad

To: Dad123@homeplace.com

The school is buying computers for the library! That makes me very happy, Dad!

Mom talked to Ms. Lovejoy, and now Mom wants me to go to the library after school every day. She wants me to do my homework there. She says that I stay up too late when I do homework at home. She is going to pick me up at the library every day. I hate the library. And I also hate fish. Mom is cooking fish for dinner tonight!

Love, Melissa

To: Melissa@eduplace.edu

This will be a short e-mail. I'm sorry about the fish, but listen to your mother. Go to the library after school. She is doing what is best for you.

Love, Dad

To: Dad123@homeplace.com

Okay, Dad.

I love you.

Melissa

To: Dad123@homeplace.com

Dad, I have another friend. Her name is Tammy. Katy, Tammy, and I go to the library together after school. We read and do our homework. Then our moms pick us up. It's fun.

The librarian, Mr. Smitz, is more interested in science-fiction books than computers. He also knows a lot of interesting things. He told us that some birds stay "married" for life. Did you know that?

Love, Melissa

To: Dad123@homeplace.com

Katy, Tammy, and I help at the library now. We put the returned books back on the shelves. Mr. Smitz talks to us about science-fiction books. He wants us to read his favorite books. I told him I don't like science fiction. I don't want to read books about robots and computers. I haven't had an e-mail from you in a long time. Please write!

Love, Melissa

November

To: Melissa@eduplace.edu

Hi, Sweetie! I'm sorry I haven't written for a while. I had a lot of work this week. I stayed late at the office almost every night. I think you are doing great! Mr. Smitz sounds like a very interesting man. I saw your friend Kendra from your old school. She says, "Hi!" She wants to see you when you visit. I can't wait for your winter vacation!

Your loving Dad

To: Dad123@homeplace.com

Mr. Smitz says, "Hi." He showed me how to find books in the library. Guess what? Mr. Smitz doesn't know how to find books on the computer. I'm going to show him how to search the Internet for books. I told Mom that Mr. Smitz is nice. I think she's going to invite him to dinner. I hope we don't have fish!

Love, Melissa

To: Dad123@homeplace.com

Mr. Smitz came to dinner. We didn't have fish. We had pizza, my favorite food! Mom and Mr. Smitz didn't talk about libraries.

That night I had a dream that Mr. Smitz was my stepfather. I don't want a new father! You are my father. I told Mom about the bad dream. She said, "Don't worry." Then she told me not to tell Mr. Smitz about the dream.

Love, Melissa

To: Melissa@eduplace.edu

Your dream sounds strange. I understand why it scared you. But don't worry. I am your father and I will always be your father. Sweetie, you can visit me in the city whenever you want. Don't eat too much fish.

Much love, Dad

To: Dad123@homeplace.com

Ms. Lovejoy says we all have to write three-page book reports! We have to give the reports to her after vacation. At my old school, we only had to write one page. It's not fair! I wanted to write about ducks. I've read all the duck books in the library. But Ms. Lovejoy says I have to read a new book. Do you have any ideas?

Love, Melissa

To: Melissa@eduplace.edu

I have many ideas, my dear. But I don't know what books are right for you. Ask Mr. Smitz. Maybe he has some good ideas. You can tell him very politely, "No science fiction, please."

Love, Dad

THREE PAGE
BOOK REPOR
DU

To: Dad123@homeplace.com

I told Mr. Smitz about our e-mails, and he thought of a book for my book report. The book is about a boy who writes letters to his favorite author. I started reading it today and I like it a lot. Now I have a book to write about.

Love, Melissa

To: Dad123@homeplace.com

The book report was fun. The book Mr. Smitz gave me was great! The report was easy to write and I liked writing it. It didn't seem like work at all.

I miss you a lot. What are we going to do when I visit you? I want to do a lot of things. Can we see a show? Can we take a walk and look at the store windows? I want to see all my friends too. And I really want to see Grandma. But most of all, I want to be with you.

Love, Melissa

December

To: Melissa@eduplace.edu

Sweetie, we're going to spend a lot of time together. We can see a show, and Grandma can come with us. I would love to take a long walk with you and your friend Kendra. Would you like to go to the zoo? Maybe we'll see wood ducks there.

Love, Dad

To: Dad123@homeplace.com

I can't wait to see you!

Love, Melissa

To: Melissa@eduplace.edu

I can't wait to see you either!

Love, Dad